Bernard the Ferret

Happy to be Himself

by Eve Stebbing

Illustrations
Cate Agnew

An imprint of Spin-Off Books
35 Bury Street
Norwich
NR2 2DJ

First Published in Great Britain by Spin-Off Books
July 16

Copyright © 2012

ISBN 9780956862211

Set in Hobo STD

Printed by Lightning Source Books Ltd.

Acknowledgements

With thanks to Bill Bufford, Spin-Off Theatre, the Ballards and the Nunziatina gang.

This book is dedicated to ferret lovers everywhere, and all those who follow in the black footed footsteps of Bernard.

The Story Begins...

Bernard was a rare,
black footed prairie
ferret.

In Norfolk where he
lived, he was not just
rare, but super-rare.

Bernard

He was a real one-off

They lived with a vicar whose house was next to the church. He was called Bill and he used to let them sit on his shoulders at night to watch the television.

For his work, Bill had to wear a stiff collar which went all the way round. It was called a dog collar. But at night, he let the ferrets drape themselves around his neck.

By day Bill had a dog collar
and by night a ferret collar.
But the ferret one was
better because it was a
ferret. The dog collar was
not a dog.

The three ferrets
who lived with
Bernard all had names...

There was Zizz
the ferret who
slept in the sock
drawer

Zizz

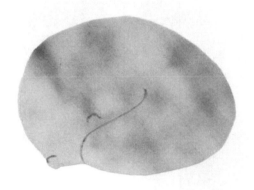

Zzzzzzzzzzzzizz

There was...

Stinker, the extra
smelly ferret

who lived in his own
box in the
conservatory.

There was Stinker

Poooeeee!

There was Ferreta
the fluffy ferret, who
looked like she'd been
frightened by a hair dryer

Zizz was sleepy, Stinker
was Smelly, Ferreta was
vain

but Bernard was BRAVE

There was Ferreta

Flufffffffffffy

One day, Stinker woke up, stretched and got out of his box. He could hear the clatter of plates in the kitchen. But he knew he wasn't allowed to join in at breakfast because he was too smelly.

He always seemed to be putting his feet in something. Wherever he went there was a pot of talcum powder or a big bar of squidgy lavender soap: things the others found really pongy.

They said he didn't smell like
a proper ferret at all.

It wasn't fair.

Stinker didn't want to be
left out any more

Today would be different

Sleepy Zizz had brought his sock to the table. He was snoring into the fruit bowl.

Ferreta was sitting on the window sill over the radiator, fluffing up after her morning shower

Bernard was patrolling the area for raisins. He loved raisins, although he knew they gave him hiccups.

Any minute now Bill might notice what he was up to and tell him off...

but Bill wasn't looking at Bernard.

Suddenly, they all looked up.

"What's that smell?" said Bill.

"What's that smell?" snuffled Zizz.

"What's that smell?"

Ferreta lifted up her fluffy locks in case it could make them dirty.

Then they saw him...

"Ooo, it's Stinker!" Squeaked Ferreta. "Urgh, he stinks."

Zizz pointed his pointy nose at Stinker,
"it's the nasty, smelly ferret, he smells like a horrid old lavender bag."

Bill opened all the windows,
but as breakfast was over,
and the room was full of

SMELL

All the ferrets left.

Stinker was on his own.
Poor Stinker.

Later that day, Bernard
was playing in the kitchen
compost bin.
He was looking for
something rotten and
festering to wear as a
ferret perfume

Suddenly, he heard a
sound...

Boooooooooooooo0
　　　　　Hoooooooooooooo

Somebody sounded very
upset. Who was it?

He crawled out of the bin
and went to look.
He went pattering across
the kitchen floor.

Patter
Patter patter

He went underneath the
conservatory door.

Squeeze, squeeze
squeeze

Then he saw an
old piece of pipe.

Stinker's tears were coming
out of the end of it.

"I used to think Stinker
was a nice name, but now
I see that it isn't."
"Yes it is" Bernard replied.

"It isn't! Nobody likes
a Stinker."
"I do," said Bernard.
"You do?"
"Yes."
"But do you think I
smell?"
"Yes I do. I think you
smell lovely..."

"Like an old piece of fish," said Bernard, sniffing his drain soaked coat... "or perhaps a bit of mouldy cheese... or maybe a fourteen day old sock."

Bernard's eyes grew bright

and his nose twitched from
side to side.   He'd had an
idea...

"Let's play a game" he
said "here, jump in that sock."

Then he called out...

"Ferrets, I have a challenge for
you! I want you to come and
experience the lovely smell
of all these socks. They're
quite terrific."

Everybody bundled up...
they all sniffed the first
sock.

"MMMM, Cheesey Feet!"
said Zizz

They all sniffed the second
sock.

"MMmm, beef pie and
vinegar" said Ferreta.

They all sniffed the third
sock with Stinker in it.
It was wriggling slightly,
but they didn't notice,
because they were so
excited by all the different
things they had sniffed.

"I'm starting to feel a bit
wizzy," said Zizz.

There was a pause.

"I know that smell" said
Zizz, "it's familiar." They
sniffed again,

"it's quite amazing."

Ferreta was so carried
away, that she stuck her
nose up the ribbing to get
a better whiff. She went
nose to nose with Stinker.
A ferret kiss.

Bernard revealed the
smelly ferret.
  "Oh, it's you!" said Zizz.
"You know, you really do
smell very nice."
  "Yes," said Ferreta, "I
think we've always been
wrong about you."

"Do you think I smell like Roses?"

"No. I think you smell like a fourteen day old sock."

"Yes" said Zizz. "A real Stinker!"

"Exactly," said Bernard. "And that's why we love you."

CPSIA information can be obtained
at www.ICGtesting.com
Printed in the USA
LVIW011540220812

2984LVUK00003B

9780956862211